H&S
2012

RAINBOW

A look at vinyl album covers from Iran

Collected by Kourosh Beigpour

RAINBOW

A look at vinyl album covers from Iran

Collected by Kourosh Beigpour

Layout: K-B-STUDIO

ISBN: 978-1-78083-146-6

Cover: Kourosh Beigpour

Kourosh Beigpour of this work in accordance with Section 77 of the Copyright, Design and Patents Act 1988

© Kourosh Beigpour

Translator: Daryoush Mohammad Poor

Kourosh Beigpour is hereby identified from Iran

Rainbow, a look at vinyl album covers from Iran

Thanks to effort of

Azita Naser Azari, Shirin Azarakhshi, Ali Abolkhayrian, Fatemeh Najari, Shahriar Shahedi, Parisa Najari,

Saeed Malek, Mostafa Owji, Kourosh Parsanezhad, Amir mansur, Sepide Chaman Ara, Babak Chaman Ara, Jalil Heydari,

Mohammad Tolouei. Qhobad Shiva, Majid Kashani, Reaza Kabiri Zad, Keyvan jafari Chaman Ara, Mohammad Reza Darvishi,

Shadab dadgar, Azin Farmandi, Abbas Chin Zhian, Samaneh Etesami, Bahman Riazi far, Alireza Nezhat Afzudi, Hossein Setareh

Introduction

This collection is an attempt to revive and recall a neglected part of the cultural experiences of Iran between the years 1959 to 1976 which are episodes of the contemporary visual art culture. Covers of gramophone records are a massive exhibition for learning about encounters with cultural commodities and revisiting how to encounter the audience. It appears that in the previous tradition of these works, people have had a serious, continuous and effective role in them from the time a work is produced, from its recording to its dissemination; and it did not matter whether the work was supposed to be pop music or special works such as the poetry of Shamlou. In both genres, the audience was always taken into account and the commodity was produced and sent to the market according to the audience demand; this attitude could hardly be seen today in similar cases.

Unfortunately, in Iran, the production of gramophone records has been completely discontinued and replaced with cassette tapes and later CD ROMs, for strange reasons which could be traced in many instances. Nonetheless, the production of records still continues to dates and many listeners prefer the warmth of the record sound to the digital systems of today. Yet, as a result of this new trend, for the exception of very few people who truly value records, all of them have either gone to dust bins or are buried in the basements; no one pays attention to the content of the works or their covers.

In this book, the effort was made to choose the best of all the existing genres and collect them in three different chapters. The focus of this book is only on the cover of these records, but in order to document, recognise and pay due respect to all those who have contributed to the production of these works, full details of them have been typed and reproduced below them in exactly the same manner that they were on the original sample. In cases where the words designer, design or painter has been used, this book represents them as they have been.

Any sloppiness in producing full details of certain works as compared with others goes entirely back to the producing company and their lack of attention to this important aspect.

The first chapter includes works in which photography has been used and mainly photographs have been the background for creating the cover. These are sometimes simple photos and sometimes collages or a combination of both. In the second chapter, the focus is on works which have been designed with the 'imagery' technique and are basically in two categories: in the first category, it is only the imagery itself which is developed by the designer and in the second, the text and typography is also reflected in the work.

Finally, the last chapter deals with typography in these works. In fact, the works in this section are created with a further emphasis on Persian script. Sometimes it is only 'calligraphy' of the script which has been the main feature of the designer's work and sometimes it even becomes the most important aspect of it. In this chapter, if a certain work has paid particular attention to the script or text even in simple names, they have been added to the collection as samples.

Chapter One

Recorded voice has been one of the intriguing attractions of this century and a product of contemporary technology. It is presented to us in new forms and different formats every day; from wax cylinders to digital machines and it continues its life.

The label of the page of the statements of Muzaffar al-Din Shah

The logo of "His Masters Voice" Company

In Iran, the first experiences in recording voices happen at the time of Nasir al-Din Shah. In his third trip to Europe, he became acquainted with a voice recording device called the 'phonograph'. This device could record and play sounds using wax cylinders and until the end of the reign of Nasir al-Din Shah it was only used exclusively for the royalty. However, since the early years of the reign of Muzaffar al-Din Shah, a limited number of these devices were brought to Iran and when cheaper devices were made, wealthier families purchased them. Later models of this device had a mandrel and a 36cm brass trumpet which could record and play sound for two minutes.

In his accounts of his second trip to Europe, Muzaffar al-Din Shah mentions having seen and purchased this device and since the early time of his reign one can trace phonographs in some homes. In this period, some of the court members who associated with musicians started recording their work.

Taherzadeh, the famous vocalist of the Qajar period, writes, "At that time, a device was brought to Iran which was called a phonograph and sound count be recorded on its cylinders and the same sound could be listened to again. Husam al-Saltana had procured one of these devices. This device was my best teacher, because I could hear my own voice and correct it wherever it needed improvement." [1]

Generally, gramophone records came into use before the Constitutional Revolutions in Iran around 1323/1905. In this same year, when Muzaffar al-Din Shah had travelled to Europe for

O Great Minister (Atabak-i A'zam), we are satisfied and happy with all the honest and valuable services you have rendered to us particularly during these three or four years that you have been holding the officer of Great Minister. God willing, we shall recompense for all of these serviced graciously and you will also not waver in your services even to the smallest degree, God willing. Be aware of our gracious opinion of yourself to the highest degree and God willing, we hope that after you have served for four hundred years, of course the Almighty will also reward you for your services. And these rewards will be given by God himself and by me, being God's shadow. We are happy with all the ministers and you do give a very good account of their services truly and in a timely fashion.

The text of the statements of Muzaffar al-Din Shah in the extant record of his voice

The record of the Poloyphone Company with the voice of Qamar al-Muluk Vaziri

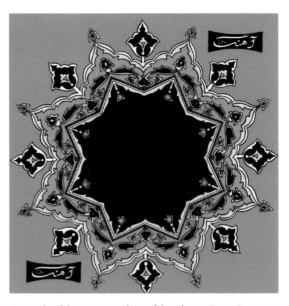

A sample of the paper envelope of the Ahange Rouz Company

treatments, he signs and seals a royal decree in January 1906 which facilitates the promotion and sales of gramophones in Iran. Following the issuing of the first decree, the first branch of sales and dissemination was established in Iran in 1906 by the "Gramaphone and Typewriter" company (Gramafon wa mashin tahrir) and the recording and production of records from the work of Iranian musicians began. Then, following the recordings, the master records were sent to one of the branches which had the facilities of mass production outside Iran and after their mass production they were disseminated inside Iran [2]. The first recorded sounds of this period are five records of the voice of the Shah and senior ministers and from these five records, three are intact (voices of Muzaffar al-Din Shah, Atabak-i A'zam and the Foreign Minister). The first music records of Muzaffar al-Din Shah's period are recorded and disseminated by the Gramaphone Company in Britain.

A branch of this company was opened in Iran in 1907 and it recorded works by Mirza Abdollah, Bagher Khan Rameshgar, Nayeb Asadollah Isfahani and also works by the Military Orchestra of the Darulfunoun School conducted by Monsieur Lumiere [1]. The first gramophone in Iran was used for the public use in front of a coffee shop on the eastern side of the Shams al-Imarah square and it is here that the gramophone is publicly introduced to the people.

This phenomenon was welcome by the interested people since it was introducing the voice of vocalists;

however, there was initially some resistance and some did not approve of its use. The first witnesses to the playing of music were coffee shop owners and coffee shop spaces. In most of these cases, the devices were often broken or the sounds heard from them were not normal and these were all results of the unfamiliarity of these people with the device [3]. The recording of works and the production of these records continued until a short while after the First World War and after a long period of cessation with the outbreak of war, it was only resumed during the Pahlavi regime. Initial records were made between 1906 and 1915 and the second period began from about 1927 continuing till the end of the second Pahlavi monarch and shortly after cassette tapes became common in Iran [4]. In the meantime, as Ahmad Shah left for Europe and Reza Khan rose to power, a new era began in the recording of works of music. Centres for the teaching of music were founded including the Darvish School under the management of Morteza Ney Davoud. One can also mention the establishment of the High School of Music in 1923 and the Musical Club by Colonel Alinaghi Vaziri and all of these provided a good atmosphere for recording and disseminating music records.

In this period, numerous concerts of musical performance were one of the reasons for attracting foreign companies to invest and send representatives for the recording and sale of records. For example, at this time, during this period, there were two active companies in Iran called His Masters Voice and Polyphon which were rivals. Both of these companies had brought a special device to Tehran for recording to make a few records of the voice of the famous vocalist of the time, Qamar al-Muluk Vaziri.

As the technology of making gramophones developed, electrical recordings were also made possible which was quite an important step in better recording sounds. The gramophone record of the first violin of Master Saba was among these records. Following the work of the aforementioned companies, other companies began recording the music work of Iranian musicians.

The names of the companies which recorded and disseminated works of music from 1927 until about 12 years later are as follows:
Bidaphone, Polyphon, Parlophon, Odeon, His Masters Voice, Columbia and Sodova

Until 1958, all details of the record were printed on the circular label in the middle of the record and the record itself was placed in a plain white envelope and it reached the customer

The CIDCYA logo

Ahange Rouz logo

in this condition [1]. However, after a while, the title of the work was written in monochrome Nastaliq calligraphy on the envelope. After a while, the task of the design on the envelopes was given to makers of rotogravures and printers and designs were often basic images of vocalists or landscapes.

Gradually, as the printing industry developed, and the public further welcomed the work, on can see further competition and the artistic value of the works leading to the improvement of the 'cover designs'. It is as of 1959 that designers such as Muhammad Bahrami and initially competent painters like Nusratullah Shirazi and Muhammad Tajvidi enter the field giving cover designs an ambience of painting and this trend reaches its climax with the huge productions made by the Ahange

Rouz Company under the management of Karim Chamanara and the Centre for Intellectual Development of Children and Young Adults (CIDCYA).

1. Shafiee, Firouz, Arayish-i Khursheed, Nishan Magazine, vol. 12, Winter 1385 Sh./2006

2. www.persiandiscography.com

3. Shahri, Ja'far, Tarikhe ejtemaee Tehran dar gharne 13 (Tehran's Social History in the 13th Century), Vol. 3, Esmailian Publishers, 1369 Sh./1990

4. Sepanta, Sasan, Tarikh Tahavvole Zabte Mousighi dar Iran (The History of the Development of Music Recording in Iran), Nima Publishers

Chapter Two

Generally, in Iran, visual approaches to gramophone records could be classified into the following categories:

1. Photographs;
2. Imagery;
3. Typography

As mentioned earlier, initial methods were more than anything else works of painters and there was no central attitude towards doing the work but some elements of a uniform approach to producing the works could be traced in all of them. For example, one can look at the example of the three volume collection of the works of Delkash with a uniform design as produced by the Ahang Company.

The highest point of designs on gramophone records happens in the 1970s. On one hand, one can mention the Ahange Rouz Company and the Centre for Intellectual Development of Children and Young Adults whose audio department was run under the management of Ahmad Reza Ahmadi and on the other hand one can mention companies such as Lavi, Caspian, Sourena, Apolon, etc.

Generally, public reception of gramophone records and its remarkable growth in this period depended on two major factors:

1. The prevailing atmosphere in the West and Western music and the simultaneous production of these works in Iran which was often done by the Ahange Rouz.

2. The productions of the Centre for Intellectual Development of Children and Young Adults and the dominant political atmosphere in it which attracted many artists.

Among all the works of this period, the CIDCYA with designers such as Farshid Mesghali, Mohammad Reza Adnani, Bahram Khaef, Ebrahim Haghighi, Mostafa Owji and a number of other designers and on the other hand the CIDCYA with its powerful management have the upper hand compared to all other companies.

1.Photographs

This part comprises many works and as many listeners of Pop music were interested in seeing the face of their favourite singers, we see numerous examples of this practice by various companies.

Among these works, the Ahange Rouz Company had a collection of Iranian Music Soloists selected and chosen as per the recommendations of Karim Chamanara, which provided coherent and unified samples to its listeners. In the second round of the production of these works, one can come up with a rare collection which is still quite valuable as compared with the current circumstances.

In this period, the Ahange Rouz Company introduces a novel initiative and courageously suggests designs for the cover of albums which are quite bold and unique in their own turn. These include the choice of carpet designs by Rassam Arabzadeh for the covers. In these kinds of works, sometimes creative and innovative approaches to photographs appear. As an example, one can look at the cover of the "Ayeneha" (Mirrors) record by Farhad which distinguishes it from other works with its silver print; or the cover of a record by Darvish Javidan, in which the figure of the photograph is quite interesting.

2.Imagery

In this method, the CIDCYA goes far ahead of all other companies using competent designers such as Soudabeh Agah, Bahram Khaef and Farshid Mesghali, producing some of the best cover designs for records. For example, pne can mention the "Nima Youshij" record with Soudabeh Agah's design, the "Ahangha-yi Mahalli" (Folk Songs) with Bahram Khaef's design inspired by the lithography ambience and the image designs of Farhid Mesghali in "She'r wa Seda-yi Ahmad Shamlou" (Ahmad Shamlou's Voice and Poetry).

However, regardless of the atmosphere of the CIDCYA, other institutes were also producing other works using designers such as Ghobad Shiva with his designs for "Shahr-i Ghesseh" and "Ostadan Moosighi-yi Sonnati-yi Iran", Parviz Kalantari's work for Samin Baghtcheban's "Rangin Kaman" or the imageries of Ahmad Sakhavarz for the Ahange Rouz Company in the "Yeki Book Yeki Nabood" collection.

Simultaneously and in line with the same approach to designs, there were other examples of realistic imageries on film posters and signs at the entrance of cinemas. Imageries for the cover of the sound track of the "Hasan Kachal", "Panjereh" or "Reza Motori" films are among samples of this kind of work.

3.Typography

In this genre of works, there have been some experiences taking into account the capacity and the potentials of the Persian calligraphy. Samples of these experiments are among the best cover designs for records. This approach to design is not exactly, in the contemporary sense of the word, typography; it is rather an attempt for representing and depicting the ambience of the work by choosing the kind of font and its different compositions.

For sure, the best examples of this genre are provided by the Lavi Company in the "Hafteh-yi Khakestari" with Mostafa Owji's calligraphy. Being familiar with the content of this work, one can easily make connections between the content and the form and composition in the design. Likewise, the CIDCYA also tries works in which Owji's influence is quite palpable; as in the "Hafez-i Shiraz" record or the poems of "Abu Saeed Abulkhayr" and in most of these works traditional calligraphic styles such as Thulth, Shikasta Nastaliq and even Persian Kufic styles are remarkably present.

A different approach to this genre can be seen in the "Bon Bast" record. Bearing in mind the decade in which the work has been produced, one can compare it with foreign works contemporary to it in terms of the use of fonts.

In the works of the CIDCYA, sometimes three names are seen on the back of the cover. One belongs to the designer, the other is the imagery artists and the third one is the calligrapher. And it is this professional approach to it which makes these kinds of works unique and unrepeatable. Sometimes the role of a knowledgeable manager like Ahmad Reza Ahmadi for the CIDCYA or Chamanara for the Ahange Rouz can transform an institute or an organisation to such a degree that they devote chapters of the contemporary cultural history to themselves.

In any event, it is sometimes necessary to look back to the past and remember previous samples of works so that they are neither forgotten nor ignored in the busy atmosphere of digital life.

Kourosh Beigpour
2011

Photographs

Chaprter One

غم تنهائی اسیرت میکنه

فریدون فروغی

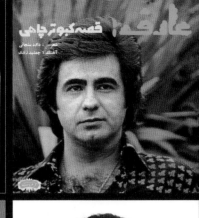

عاشق قصه کبوتر چاهی

ماه پیشونی

سفر

هدیه اردلان سرفراز و حسن شماعی‌زاده

آسمون با من وتو قهره دیگه

آپولون

آوازخیم زن باکره

فریدون فروغی

زندگی و آثار
چایکوفسکی
نوشته‌ی ارسلان ساسانی، نقاشی هوشنگ محمدیان

- **Life and Works 9 |** Tchaikovsky
Painting: Houshang Mohammadian

Produced by the CIDCYA 1975

Text: Arsalan Sasani
Voice: Muzaffar Moghaddam, Mahin Nathri, Pirouz Chehrehnegar, Bagher Karimpour, Hossein Vaezi, Sadruddin Shajareh, Khosrow Farzadi

● **Cover design and back design of Avazha-yi Emrouz**
Design: Farshid Mesghali
Photo: Masoud Masoumi

Produced by the CIDCYA 1975

Music: Ramin Entezami | Vocalist: Pari Zanganeh |
Poem by: M. Azad, Houshang Ebtehaj, Yadollah Royai,
Farhad Sheibani, Mehdi Akhavan Salles, Sohrab Sepehri

تهیه شده در کانون پرورش فکری کودکان و ن
تهران ۱۳۵۴ قیمت :

● **Darvazeh (The Gate) |** Film Sound Track

Produced by the CIDCYA 1975

Composer: Esfandiar Monfaredzadeh | Director: Yan Onk

• Mah Pishooni "Ghesseye Malek Jamshid" (Moon-like forhead – The Story of King Jamshid)| Film Sound Track
Cover design: Fereydoon Farrokhzad

Produced by Ahange Rouz

Cast: Nazi, Setareh (Mah Pishooni), Amir Fakhreddin (Malek Jamshid), Raziani (Soheil Jadougar), Parvin Malakouti (Zivar Khanoom – Zan Baba), Maryam Parvin (Golrokh), Habibullah Bolour (Amir), Jamshid Mehrdad (Vazir), Yasamini (Jadougar)
Producer and Director: Dr. Koushan | Filming director: Mahmoud Koushan | Produced by Pars Film | Music: Manouchehr Goudarzi

• Iranian Birthday Song | By: Anoushiravan Rohani

Produced by Ahange Rouz

• Norouz Mubarak Bad (Happy Norouz) |
Norouz Gift of 1974, Ministry of Culture and Arts

Produced by Ahange Rouz 1974

1. Sedaye Bahar (The Sound of the Spring)| Poem: Lobat Valla | Music: Abbas Khoshdel
2. Taranehaye Mahalliye Iran (Iranian Folk Songs) | National Choir Orchestra | Conductor: Alfred Mardouyan
The Bashet Badi folk song and Kurdish folk song | Arrangement: A. Mardouyan
Gilaki folk song | Arrangement: R. Gregorian

● **Asemoun va Darya (The sky and the sea) | Shab, Man va Sange Sabour (Night, me and the patient listener)**

Produced by Ahange Rouz

Poem: Homa Mirafshar | Voice: Rezayan

• Molla mammad jan | Pouran

Produced by Ahange Rouz

Rasti che zood migzareh (Time really flies), Sobh misheh shab misheh (Dawn breaks, dusk comes), Geryeh delo safa mideh (Tears won't cure the heart), Viroon beshi ey del (May you be devastated), Migardam dore donya (I am wandering around the world), Asheghi bad dardiyeh (Being in love is tough), Vah che balaee ey del (How naughty your are, O heart of mine!), Zendegi ey zendegi (Life, O life!), Ageh misheh bargard (Please come back!), Emrouzo farad (Today and tomorrow), Haliteh (Do you understand?)

• Del migeh delbar miyad (The heart tells me the beloved is coming back) | Mahasti

Produced by Ahange Rouz

Side 1: Del migeh delbar miyad (The heart tells me the beloved is coming back), Degar che khahi (What else do you want?), Ashegh shodan bi haseleh (Falling in love is futile), Tars az jodaee (Fear of separation)
Side 2: Man digeh yar nemikham, Deleh in, Sedaye pa, Bacheh nasho ey del

• Gole Maryam | Giti

Produced by Ahange Rouz

Ta vaghti ke man bemiram del bemire (Unti I die, until the heart dies), Atishe esghe ke khamoush nemisheh (It is the flame of love that never dies), Shadi ba man ghahreh (Happiness has sulked with me), Dele man geryeh makon (Do not weep, O heart of mine!), Tasbih sad daneh (Hundred beads rosary), Del tora mikhad (The heart desires you), Divare jodaee (The wall of separation), Dele bolhavas (The mischievous heart), Ketabe gham (The book of sorrow), Rizeh rizeh (Little by little), Be man nakhand (Do not laught at me)

● **Ghame tanhaee asiret mikoneh (The pain of loneliness will enslave you)**

Producet by Studio Ballet

Music: William | Poem: Arash | Piano: Serge Gorkian | Vocalist: Fereydoun Foroughi

● **Bouye tane to (The Fragrance of Your Body)**

Produced by Monaco Stereo

Poem and music: Masoud Amini | Vocalist: Kamran

● **Hamisheh ghayeb (The Always Absent) |** For Amir Naderi for his Tangsir

Produced by Studio Lavi

Voice: Feretydoun Foroughi | Words by: Shahyar Ghanbari | Arrangement: Varouzhan

آئینه‌ها (مسخ)   فــرهـاد

● **Ayeneha (Maskh) | Metamorphosis &**
Mirror | Farhad

Music: Hasan Shamaeezadeh | Vocalist: Farhad |
Poem: Ardalan Sarafraz | Arrangement: Manouchehr Eslami

سفـــر

هـــدیـــه اردلان سرفـــراز و حسن شمـــاعـــــیزاده

- **Safar (Journey) |** A gift from Ardalan
Sarafraz and Hasan Shamaeezadeh

Produced by Caspian

نازنین ، هدیه‌ای برای تو که هر روز جمعه است

نازنین ، هدیه‌ای برای تو که هر روز جمعه است

• **Cover and back design of the Jom'eh (Friday) record |** Nazanin, A gift for you whose every day is a Friday

Farhad | Shahyar Ghanbari | Esfandiar Monfaredzadeh

• **Hou Ya Ali Madad |** Darvish Mostafa Javidan

Produced by Harmony Apolon

Vocalist, Poet and Composer: Darvish Mostafa Javidan | in association with Chogour: Foroughi Kermani
Recording engineer: Alireza Gorji | Reciter: Houshang Bashirnejad | Recorded at Studio Barbad

● **Salam bar eshgh (Hail to Love) | Bar nemigardam (I will not come back) |**
Iraj Mahdian

Produced by Studio Avayeh Shahr

Salam bar eshgh (Hail to Love) | Poem and Music: Samad Nourian | Bar nemigardam | Poem and Music: Iraj Taheri

● **Cover and back design of record: Tanha sedast ke mimanad (It is only the voice that shall last)**
Cover design: Feyedoun Farrokhzad
Cover calligraphy: Reza Mafi

Produced by Studio Avayeh Shahr

Forough mikhanad, Fereydoun mikhanad, Fereydoun Forough ra mikhanad
Music: Fariborz Lachini | Back cover: An extract of the letters of Forough to Fereydoun

● Siah va sepid (Black and White) | Shahede gham (The lovely pain)

Produced by Ahangi Rouz

Music and vocalist: Emad Ram | Poem: Moeini
Kermanshahi | Reciter: Azar Pajouhesh

Majmou'eye Tankavazane Mousighiye
Irani (Collection of Soloists of Iranian Music)

Produced by Ahange Rouz

● **Majmou'eye Tankavazane Mousighiye Irani (Collection of Soloists of Iranian Music) |** Emad Ram, Flute Soloist

Produced by Ahange Rouz

Shoushtari, Segah, Dashti, Bayate Zand | Accompanied by Amir Naser Eftetah's Tombak

غمزه   شب نشینی   محبت   عود

خلوت دل   سنتور   اشک   دلربا

انتظار   نی   گریه شمع   ویلن

پیانو   پیانو   عاشقان   اشتیاق

° Majmou'eye Tankavazane Mousighiye
rani (Collection of Soloists of Iranian Music)

Produced by Ahange Rouz

شوق   فلوت

- **Tankavazane Mousighiye Irani**
(Soloists of Iranian Music) | Violin

Produced by Ahange Rouz

Homayoun Khorram with Hossein Hamedanian's Tombak

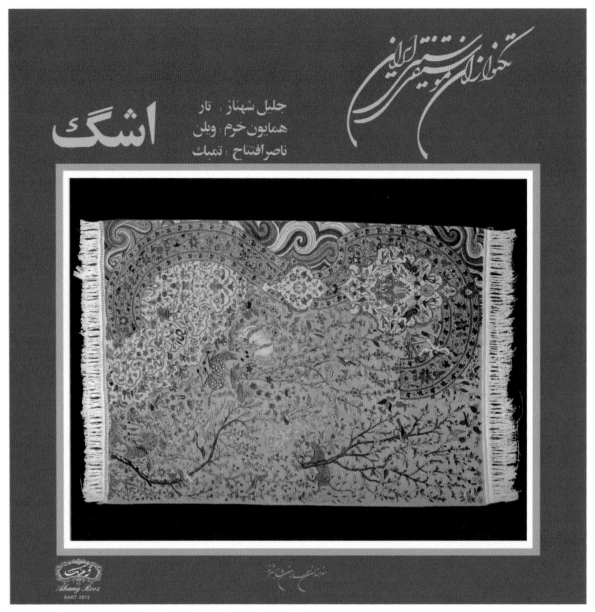

اشگ

كنوازان موسيقى ايران

جليل شهناز : تار
همايون خرم : ويلن
ناصر افتتاح : تمبك

● **Tankavazane Mousighiye Irani (Soloists of Iranian Music)** | Dashti by Homayoun Khorram

Produced by Ahange Rouz

Jalil Shahnaz: Tar | Homayoun Khorram: Violin | Naser Eftetah: Tombak
Side 1: Daramad, Chahar Mezrab, the Ashk (Tears) piece
Side 2: Gousgheye Oshagh, the Ashk piece, Mathnavi, Gilaki, Foroud, the Ashk piece

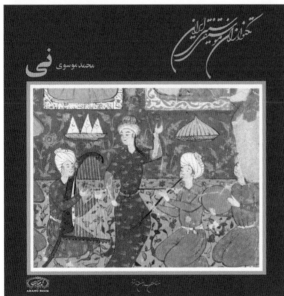

• **Tankavazane Mousighiye Irani (Soloists of Iranian Music) |** Kharabat

Produced by Ahange Rouz

Jalil Shanaz: Tar | Homayoun Khorram: Violin | Naser Eftetah: Tombak

• **Tankavazane Mousighiye Irani (Soloists of Iranian Music) |** Ghamzeh

Produced by Ahange Rouz

Jalil Shahnaz: Tar | Homayoun Khorram: Violin | Naser Eftetah: Tombak

• **Tankavazane Mousighiye Irani (Soloists of Iranian Music) |** Nay, Mohammad Mousavi

Produced by Ahange Rouz

• Souratgare Naghghashe Chin |
Composer and Piano Soloist: Javad Maroufi

Produced by Ahange Rouz

Side 1: Fantasy on the theme of "Sheida", Karevane Eshgh, Bobolan Mastand, Esfahan
Side 2: Saghi, Souratgare Naghghashe Chin, Morghe Hagh, Mastaneh

• Renghaye Shade Irani (Iranian happy themes) | Goudarzi Orchestra

Produced by Ahange Rouz

Music arrangement and performance: Manouchehr Goudarzi | with the Goudarzi Orchestra Ensemble
Side 1: Renge Baba Karam, Renge Golpari Joon, Renge Bandari, Renge Mobarak Bad, Renge Mash Mashallah
Side 2: Renge Shateri, Renge Ghasemabadi, Renge Nash Nash, Renge Attarbashi, Renge Segah, Renge Nabat, Renge Ghouchani

• Renghaye Shad on themes of Persian folk dances | Cheshmazar Orchestra

Produced by Ahange Rouz

Music arrangement and performance: Naser Chashmazar | with the Chashmazar Orchestra Ensemble
Side 1: Renge Baba Karam, Renge Choupani, Renge Shokoufeh, Renge Vaghazali, Renge Roshan, Renge Lezgi
Side 2: Renge Mobarak Bad, Renge Golchehreh, Renge Naz, Renge Shalakhou, Renge Gol, Renge Mojassameh

• Royaye Javani (The dream of youth) |
Composer and Piano Soloist: Javad Maroufi

Produced by Ahange Rouz

Side 1: Sarban, Khorshid Midarakhsha, Entezar, Khatereh'ee az Ostad

Side 2: Yad be Nazanine Safarkardeh, Royaye Javani, Arezou, Golpari joon (Folk theme)

SARP 1004

شعرهای هوشنگ ابتهاج، باصدای هوشنگ ابتهاج، تکنواز پیانو: پرویزاتابکی

• **Cover and back design for the Poet's Voice record 5** | Houshang Ebtehaj

Poems of Houshang Ebtehaj with his own voice | Piano Soloist: Parviz Atabaki

Produced by the CIDCYA 1972

شعرهای هوشنگ ابتهاج، باصدای هوشنگ ابتهاج، تکنواز پیانو: پرویز اتابکی

- **Tabrike Norouz (Norouz Felicitations)** | Baharoun (The Spring)

Produced by Ahange Rouz

Music: Parviz Atabaki | Performance by the Babak Choir Ensemble

- **Oude Man Khodahafez (Adieu my Oud) | Gham, Dooste Ghadimiey Man (Sorrow, My Old Friend) |** Abdolvahab Shahidi

Produced by Ahange Rouz

Oude Man Khodahafez | Poem: Nariman | Gham Dooste Ghadimiye Man | Poem: Homa | Reciter: Azar Pajouhesh

- **Shotorbana (O Camel Leader) | Geleh Daram (I have grievances) |** Abdolvahab Shahidi

Produced by Ahange Rouz

Nay Soloist: Hasan Nahid | Oud Soloist and Vocalist: Abdolvahab Shahidi | Music arrangement and performance: Abdolvahab Shahidi | Geleh Daram in the Nava mode | Shotorbana in the Dashtestani mode
Side 1: Geleh Daram | Poem and song by Homa Mirafshar
Side 2: Shotorbana | Poem: Mawlana Abdurrahman Jami

Chaprter Two

imagery

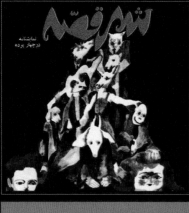

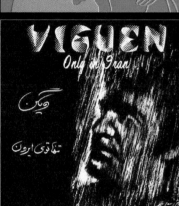

● Rosvaee (Scandal) | The song of Do ta cheshmoon (Two Eyes) | Mahasti

Produced by Apolon

Do ta cheshmoon song | Music and Orchestra: Emad Ram | Poem: Misha Javdani
Rosvaee song (Mageh Na) | Music: Sadruddin Mahvan | Poem: Touraj Negahban

روزی که خورشید
به دریا رفت

نوشته‌ی: هما سیار

موسیقی: شیدا قرچه‌داغی

● **Rouzi ke khorshid be darya raft (The day the sun went to the sea)**

Produced by the CIDCYA 1973

Text: Homa Sayyar | Music: Sheida Gharcheh Daghi
Voice: Simin Ehsasi, Reza Babak, Sousan Farrokhnia, Alireza Hodaee, Bahram Shah Mohammadlou, Shiva Gourani, Marziyeh Boroumand

• **Poet's Voice 6 |** Mehdi Akhavan Salles
Design, arrangement and painting: Farshid Mesghali

Produced by the CIDCYA 1973

Poems of Mehdi Akhavan Salles with his own voice | Music: Fereydoun Shahbazian

• **Ki az hameh por zourtareh? (Who is stronger than all?)**
Design and painting: Ebrahim Haghighi

Produced by the CIDCYA

Readaptaton: M. Azad | Music: Karim Gougerdchi

• **Aftab amad aftabe mehr amad (The sun has come; the autumn sun has come)**
Cover design: Farshid Mesghali

Produced by the CIDCYA 1975

Poem: Mowlavi, Ahmad Reza Ahmadi | Music: Daryoush Dolatshahi | Reciter: Bijan Mofid | Vocals: Choir

- **Ostadane Mousighiye Sonnatiye Iran (Masters of Persian Traditonal Music)**
Designer: Ghobad Shiva

Produced by the Ahange Rouz Company |
Commissioned by the Shiraz Art Festival
Organisation, Persepolis

Kamancheh: Asghar Bahari in the Esfahan mode | Setar by
Ebadi in the Chahargah mode | Tar by Lotfullah Majd
in the Shour mode | Solo Tombak by Hossein Tehrani
Recording by: Yousef Shahab

● **Life and Works 6 |** Schubert
Painting: Ebrahim Haghighi

Produced by the CIDCYA 1973

Text by Claude de Ferrain | Translation: Khosrwo Samiee
Reciters: Mohammad Jafari, Simin Ehsasi, Khosrwo
Farzadi, Bagher Karimpour

زندگی و آثار

شوبرت

نوشته‌ی کلود دوفرن. ترجمه‌ی خسرو سمیعی. نقاشی ابراهیم حقیقی

● **Shahre Ghesseh (The tale city) |**
Namayeshnameh dar chahar pardeh (A play in four acts)

Design: Ghobad Shiva

Produced by Ahange Rouz

An Play in Four Acts | Writer and Director: Bijan Mofid |
Storyteller: Jamileh Nedaee (Mofid)
Composer, song writer and vocalist: Bijan Mofid |
Recording: Yousef Shahab

● **Baroun Barouneh (It's rain, rain) |**
(Golnesa) Dastane yek eshght (A
romance tale) | Vigen

Cover design: Mohammad Bahrami

Produced by by Ahang

● **Poet's Voice 10 |** Poems of Sa'di recited by Houshang Ebtehaj

Design and painting: Farshid Mesghali

Produced by the CIDCYA 1973

Music: Fereydoun Shahbazian

قصّهٔ طوطی

شعر از م . آزاد

- **Seda baraya koudakan (Voices for children) 3 |** ye Toghi (Toghi's Story)
Cover design: Farshid Mesghali

Produced by the CIDCYA 1971

Poem: M. Azad | Music: Sheida Gharcheh Daghi
Voices of Nikou Kheradmand as story teller | Ahmad
Rasoulzadeh: Toghi's father | Ramin Jamshidipour: Toghi
| Naser Tahmasb: Joula Rangraz | Mehdi Ajir: Sha'rbaf Darzi

انگشتری جادو

نوشته‌ی : کنستانتین پاستوفسکی   ترجمه‌ی : پوران صلح‌کل

انگشتری جادو

شاهزاده‌ی‌شاد

نوشته : اسکار وایلد
ترجمه‌ی : فریدون معزی مقدم

• Cover and back design of Voices for Children 11 | Angoshtariye Jadou (The Magic Ring)

Design and painting by Mohammad Adnani

Produced by the CIDCYA 1972

Written by Konstantin Paustovsky | Translated by Pouran Solhe Kol
Voices of Muzffar Moghaddam as Reciter | Bahman Zarrinpour: Grandfather | Bahram Vatanparast: Old Soldier | Farah Kazemi: Varusha

• Voices for Children 9 | Shahzadeye Shad (The Happy Prince)

Produced by the CIDCYA 1972

Written by: Oscar Wilde | Translated by Fereydoun Moezzi Moghaddam
Voices of Fereydoun Daemi as the Story Teller | Jalal Maghami as the Prince | Elaheh Parsaee as the Swallow

● **Cover and back design of the Poet's**
Voice 9 record | Poems of Nader Naderpour
Designer: Farshid Mesghali
Painting: Mohammad Adnani

Produced by Ahange Rouz

Poems of Nader Naderpour | Photo: Masoud Masoumi |
Music: Karim Gougerdchi

• **Cover and back design for Poet's Voice 8** | Poems of Roudaki
Designer: Farshid Mesghali
Calligraphy: Mostafa Owji

Produced by the CIDCYA 1973

Music: Feryedoun Shahbazian | Vocalist: Pari Zanganeh | Reciter: Manouchehr Anvar

• **Majmou'eye She'r va Sedaye Sha'er | (Collections of Poetry and Poet's)**

Produced by the CIDCYA

• **Seda baraya nojavanan (Voices for Young Adults) 2** | Kouti va Mouti
Design and Painting: Mostafa Owji

Produced by the CIDCYA 1973

Written by Bijan Mofid | Music by Kambiz Roshanravan
Voices of Alireza Mojallal, Jamileh Nedaee, Bijan Mofid, Siavash Tahmoures, Ardavan Mofid, Sousan Taslimi

ماهی سیاه کوچولو

نوشته‌ی بهرنگ

- **Seda baraye koudakan (Voices for Children) 1 |** Mahi siaha kouchoulou (The Little Black Fish)

Painting: Farshid Mesghali

Produced by the CIDCYA 1971

Written by Samad Behrangi

• Shab va Divar (The Night and the Wall)

Produced by Caspian

Vocalist: Sattar | Poet: Iraj Jannati Ataei | Composer: Babak Bayat

• Naghmehaye Koudak (Children's Songs)
Design and arrangement of the cover: Ahange Rouz Production Company

Produced by Ahange Rouz 1970 | Publications of the General Bureau of Art Education

Record 1
Songs: Hasan Radmard | Poems: Ebrahim Safaee | Vocalist: Frida Tasbihi
Side 1: Arousake khosgele man (My lovely doll), Shangoulam (I am jolly), Mangoulam (I am joyful), Kalagheh (The crow)
Side 2: Sobhe Zood (Early Morning), Gorbeye Malous (The Sweet Kitten), Shirin Zaban (The Sweetspoken)
Record 2
Songs: Hasan Radmard, Habibullah Fakhim | Poems: Ebrahim Safaee , Naser Khadivi | Vocalist: Frida Tasbihi
Side 1: Sobhe Koudak (Child's Morning), Toupe Seid (The White Ball), Amou Nourouz (Uncle Norouz), Yeki Bood Yeki Nabood (Once Upon a Time)
Side 2: Joojeh (The Chicken), Koudake Ba Adab (The Polite Child), Sedaye Zang (The Soud of the Bell), Sage Pashmalou (The Hairy Dog), Moosh (The Mouse)

• Poet's Voice 7 | Poems of Shahriar with his own voice
Design and painting: Ebrahim Haghighi

Produced by the CIDCYA 1973

Poems of Shahriar with his own voice | Music: Karim Gougerdchi

شعرهای
احمدشاملو
باصدای احمدشاملو
موسیقی متن :
اسفندیارمنفودزاده

- **Cover and back design of Poet's Voice 3 |** Poems of Ahmad Shamlou **Design and painting: Farshid Mesghali**

Produced by the CIDCYA 1972

Poems of Ahmad Shamlou with his own voice | Music Esfandiar Monfaredzadeh

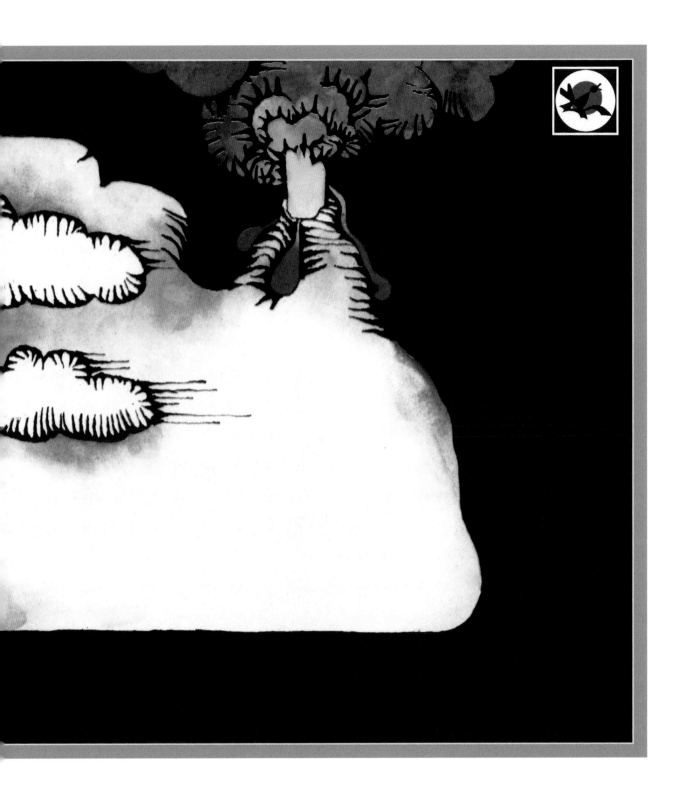

• Haft Sine Norouzi (The Seven 'Seen's for Norouz) | Amou Norouz

Produced by Ahange Rouz

• Cover and back design of the Rangin Kaman (Rainbow) record | Samin Baghtcheban

Painting: Parviz Kalantari

Performances by members of the Radio Vienna Symphonic Orchestra
Conductor: Thomas Christian David | Mitra Choir |
Conductor: Evelin Baghtcheban | Bahjat Ghasri: Soprano
Evelin Baghtcheban: Mezzo-soprano
Side 1: Norouz tou rahe (The Norouz is on its way),
Rouze barf baziyeh (It is the day for playing with snow),
Gonjiskho barfo baron (The sparrow, the snow and the rain), Trane ghashange man (My beautiful train), Jaye ahou (The deer's place), Gorbei ke madare (The cat who is a mother)
Side 2: Korange bala (The Naughty Korang), Aroosake joon (Dear Doll), Panj ta naghghashi (Five Paintings), Baghe ma parchin dareh (Our garden has a fence)

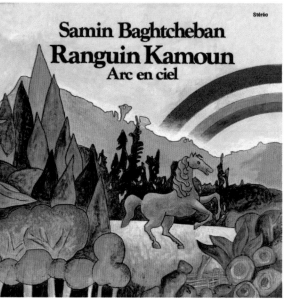

● **Inside page of the book – The Rangin Kaman (Rainbow) record**

● **Cover and back design of the Khooneh (Home) record** | Dariush

Poem: Iraj Jannati Ataei | Music: Babak Bayat | Arrangement: Oshal

Produced by Caspian

۱ زندگی و آثار
نوشته‌ی: کلود دوفرن
ترجمه‌ی: محمد قاضی
نقاشی: مصطفی اوجی

۲ زندگی و آثار بتهوون
نوشته‌ی: زاک برادر ٭ ترجمه‌ی: محمد قاضی ٭ نقاشی: سودابه ۲گاه

زندگی و آثار موزار
نوشته‌ی: ژرژ دوهامل
ترجمه‌ی: لیلی امیر ارجمند
نقاشی: مصطفی اوجی

زندگی و آثار ابوالحسن صبا
با صدای فیروز ابراهیمی

زندگی و آثار باخ
نوشته‌ی ایزیدور خروسمیعی نقاشی: مصطفی اوجی

زندگی و آثار شوبرت
نوشته‌ی کلود دوفرن، ترجمه‌ی خسروسمیعی، نقاشی ابراهیم حقیقی

زندگی و آثار ویوالدی
نوشته‌ی والـدری
ترجمه‌ی بیرخ‌منطقی
نقاشی ام‌محمدرضا عبدالی

فرانتس لیست
نوشته‌ی اودوویر ترجمه‌ی خسروسمیعی نقاشی ام‌محمدرضا عبدالی

چایکوفسکی

امیرحسین

- **Life and Works 7 |** Vivaldi
Painting: Mohammad Reza Adnani

Produced by the CIDCYA 1973

Antonio Vivaldi | Written by: Jean Roy | Translated by
Behrokh Montazami
Voices of Simin Ehsasi, Khosrwo Farzadi, Alireza
Mojallal, Mohammad Jafari

• Tanha tooye Iroon (Alone in Iran) | Vigen

Part 1: Akse man (My picture), Kasachouk, Sholeh (The Flame), Tanha tooye Iroon (Alone in Iran), Marde Sargardoun (The Wandering Man)
Part 2: Shadoumad (The Bridegroom), Gole Sorkh (The Red Rose), Biganeh Bia (Come, O stranger!), Dele divaneh (The Crazy Heart), Lalaee (The Lullaby)

• Life and Works 4 | Abolhasan Saba
Designer: Farshid Mesghali

Produced by the CIDCYA 1973

Abolhasan Saba | Voice of Firouzeh Amir Moezz

• Del migeh delbar miyad (The Heart Says the Beloved is Coming) | Be man nagoo doostet daram (Don't tell me you love me) | Fukahi (Satire)

Produced by Harmony Apolon

Vocalist and Poet: Fakour

سلی

اشارتهای دل
بهت نگفتم

• **Esharathaye del (Beckonings of the Heart) | Behet nagoftam (Didn't I tell you) |** Soli

Produced by Royal

Music: Parviz Atabaki | Poem: Mohammad Malmir | Vocalist: Soli

• Zendoone del (The Heart's Prison) | Fereydoun Foroughi

Produced by Juliet

Poem and music: William Kheno | Piano: Manouchehr Chashmazar | Vocal: Fereydoun Foroughi

• Ghesseh (The Tale) | Gohar Yekdaneh (The Unique Pearl) | touraj

Produced by Royal Sourena

Ghesseh (The Tale) | Voice and Music: Touraj | Poem: Shabob | Arrangement: Eric
Gohare Yekdaneh (The Unique Pearl) | Voice and Music: Touraj | Poem: Hafez | Arrangement: Eric

• Perspolis barandeh mishe (Perspolis shall win)
Design: Hossein Asghar's Art Atelier

Music: Manouchehr Salahshour | Poem: Abolfazl Adabi | Vocalist: Firouz Berenjianh

دریاچه قو

یک باله از چایکوفسکی

نوشته‌ی فرانسیس اسکالیا

ترجمه‌ی بیژن خرسند

صدای مظفر مقدم

● **Cover and back design of the Swan Lake record |** Tchaikovsky
Design and Painting: Bahjat Poushanchi

Produced by the CIDCYA 1972

Written by: Francis Scalia | Translated by Bijan Khorsand
Voice of Muzaffar Moghaddam

طرح و نقاشی از بهجت یوسفی

قصه‌ی
فندق‌شکن
یک باله از چایکوفسکی

نوشته‌ی : ای . تی . ا . هافمن

ترجمه‌ی : پوران صلح‌کل

• The Nutcracker | Tchaikovsky
Design and Painting: Bahjat Poushanchi

Produced by the CIDCYA 1972

Written by Ernst Theodor Amadeus Hoffmann | Translated
by Pouran Solhe Kol | Voice of Muzffar Moghaddam

• Atal Matal

Produced by the CIDCYA 1974

Poem arrangement: Nouruddin Zarrinkelk | Music: Kambiz Roshanravan | Reciter: Shiva Gourani

• Ghesseye Kerme Abrisham (The Caterpillar Tale)
Painting by Nouruddin Zarrinkelk | Design by Setareh Sanj

Produced by the CIDCYA 1974

Written by Nouruddin Zarrinkelk | Music: Hossein Alizadeh Voice of Jamileh Nedaee, Sousan Taslimi, Mitra Ghamsari, Shima Mofid

• Avazhaye Koudakan (Children's Singing)

Produced by the CIDCYA 1974

Arrangement of songs: Hossein Alizadeh | Poem: Hamid Hamzeh
Hungarian Dance, Songs of Brahms, One pieace | Behrouz Dabir Moghaddam, Mohsen Mesbahi
Kermanshahi Folk Song, Italian Folk Song, Bandari Folk Song, English Folk Song, Mojdeh | Hossein Alizadeh
The music of this record has been perfomed by the children of library 18 of the CIDCYA in Tehran.

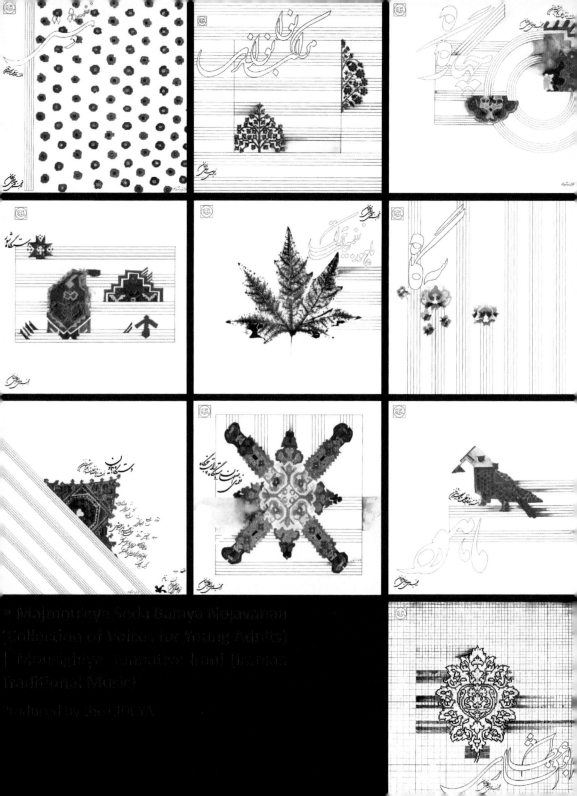

● Majmou'eye Soda Baraya Nojavanan
(Collection of Voices for Young Adults)
| Mousighye Sonnatye Irani (Iranian
Traditional Music)

Produced by the CIDCYA

- **Naghmeye Esfahan (Esfahan Song) | Dastgahe Rastpanjgah (The Rastpanjgah Modality)**
Cover design: Farshid Mesghali

Produced by the CIDCYA 1975

Text, selection and supervision by Kambiz Roshanravan
Vocalist: Mohammad Reza Shajarian | Poem of the chant:
Mowlavi | Reciter: Nikou Kheradmand | Recording by Iraj
Haghighi

Santour: Esmail Tehrani | Tar: Houshang Zarif | Setar:
Mehrbanou Tofigh | Kamancheh: Rahmatullah Badiee |
Oud: Mohammad Delnavazi
Players of the Esfahan Song | Rahatullah Badiee:
Kamancheh | Esmail Tehrani: Santour | Davoud
Vaseghi: Tombak | Kazem Alemi: Tar | Mohammad
Delnavazi: Oud

شبانه

کلام

فرهاد   احمد شاملو   اسفندیار منفردزاده

دکتر صلحی‌زاده   به دکتر غلامحسین ساعدی   به دکتر اسماعیل خوئی

● **Cover and back design of the Shabaneh (Noctural) record**
Cover design by Esfand
Produced by Lavi

Farhad | Ahmad Shamlou | Esfandiar Monfaredzadeh
To Dr. Solhizadeh | To Dr. Gholamhossein Sa'edi | To Dr. Esmail Khoi

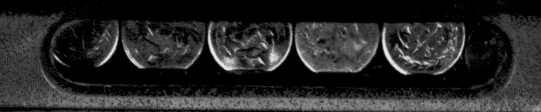

Mills BELL·O·MATIC CORP.

PAY LINE

MYSTERY

FOR   PAYS

پنج تومان

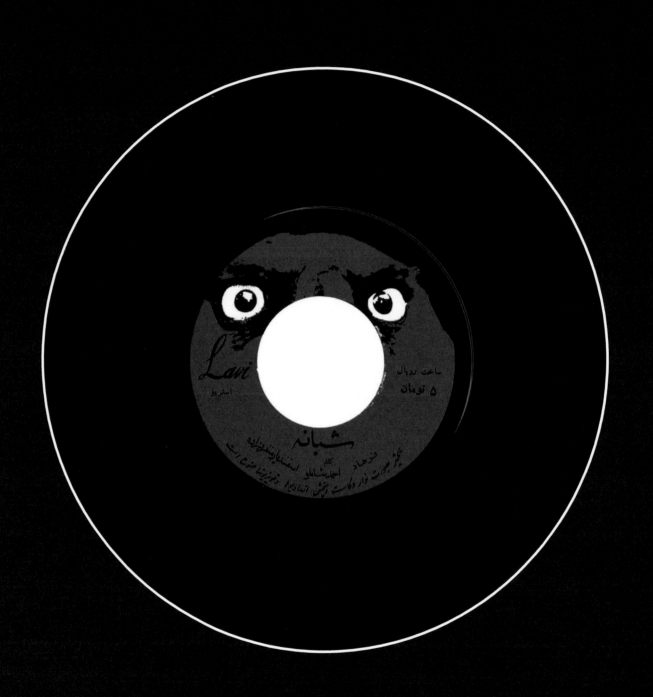

• Gorbeye Chakmehpoush (The Cat in Boots)

Tehran 1971

Translator and license holder: Faegheh Ramzi

• Sargozashte Roya (Roya's Biogaphy)

Tehran 1971

Translator and license holder: Faegheh Ramzi

• Pirzane Mehraban (The Kind Old Lady) Painting by Ahmad Sakhavarz

Produced by Ahange Rouz

A record from the series of Yeki Bood... Yeki Nabood (Once upon a time) | Under the supervision of Kioumars Derembakhsh
Poem: Jahanbakhsh Pazouki | Voices of Simin Sarkoub, Sorayya Hamidi, Pouneh, Morteza Ahmadi, Ajir | Zarb by Amir Bidarian | Recording director: Morteza Ahmadi Recording and editing by Alireza Gorji

• Arousiye Agha Moosheh va Khaleh Souskeh (The Wedding of Mr. Mouse and Mrs. Cockroach)
Painting by Ahmad Sakhavarz

Produced by Ahange Rouz

A record from the series of Yeki Bood... Yeki Nabood (Once upon a time) | Poem: Jahanbakhsh Pazouki | Voices of Simin Sarkoub, Sorayya Hamidi, Pouneh, Morteza Ahmadi, Ajir | Zarb by Amir Bidarian

• Cover and back design of the Boz Boze Ghandi (The Sugar Goatie) record
Painting by Ahmad Sakhavarz

Produced by Ahange Rouz

A record from the series of Yeki Bood... Yeki Nabood (Once upon a time) | Under the supervision of Kioumars Derembakhsh
Poem: Jahanbakhsh Pazouki | Voices of Simin Sarkoub, Sorayya Hamidi, Pouneh, Morteza Ahmadi, Ajir | Zarb by Amir Bidarian
Recording director: Morteza Ahmadi
Recording and editing by Alireza Gorji

نوشته‌ی: کلود دوفرن
ترجمه‌ی: محمدقاضی
نقاشی: مصطفی اوجی

- **Life and Works 1** | Chopin
Painting: Mostafa Owji

Produced by the CIDCYA 1972

Frédéric Chopin | Written by: Claude de Ferrain |
Translated by Mohammad Ghazi
Voice of Muzaffar Moghaddam, Khosrow Farzadi, Zhaleh

زندگی و آثار

بتهوون

نوشته‌ی: ژاک پرادر ٭ ترجمه‌ی: محمدقاضی ٭ نقاشی: سودابه آگاه

● **Life and Works 2 |** Beethoven
Painting: Soudabeh Agah

Produced by the CIDCYA 1972

Ludwig van Beethoven | Written by Jacque Pradaire |
Translated by Mohammad Ghazi
Voice of Nikou Kheradmand, Manouchehr Anvar

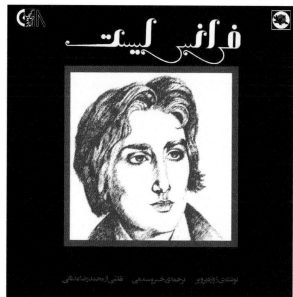

• Life and Works 5 | Bach
Painting by Mostafa Owji

Produced by the CIDCYA 1973

Johann Sebastian Bach | Written by Jacque Pradaire | Translated by Khosrow Samiee | Voice of Muzaffar Moghaddam

• Life and Works 3 | Mozart
Painting: Mostafa Owji

Produced by the CIDCYA 1972

Wolfgang Amadeus Mozart | Written by George de Hammel | Translated by Leili Amir Arjomand | Voice of Mahnouchehr Anvar

• Life and Works 8 | Franz Liszt
Painting by Mohammad Reza Adnani

Produced by the CIDCYA 1972

Franz Liszt | Written by José Bröyer | Translated by Khosrow Samiee
Voice of Mahnouchehr Anvar, Reza Babak, Sousan Farrokhnia, Naser Tahmasb, Bagher Karimpour

Inside page of the book - Bach room

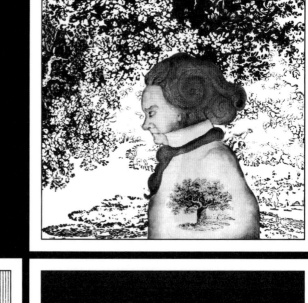

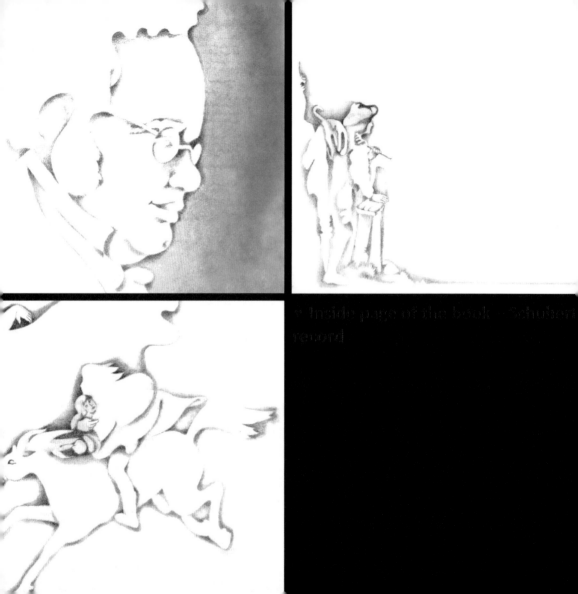

v Inside page of the book – Schubert record

قطعاتی در دستگاههای کلاسیک ایران

دلکش

دشتی۔شوشتری۔سه گاه۔بیات ترک

آهنگ

IRLP. 20001 - HI - FI

۱

● **Delkash (1) |** Pieces in Classcial Iranian Modes

Pars Gravure Making

Song made in 1959

Dashti | Lyric by Shahriar | Violin by Parviz Yahaghi
Shoushtari | Poem: Navvab Safa | Tar: Farhang Sharif
Segah| Poem: Bijan Taraghghi | Violin: Parviz Yahaghi
Bayat Tork | Lyric by Sa'di | Violin: Ali Tajvidi | Tar:
Farhang Sharif

• Geleh daram va Shotorbana (I have grievances & O camel leader)
Cover painting: Nosratullah Shirazi

Produced by Ahange Rouz

Geleh daram | Oud and vocalist: Abdolvahab Shahidi |
Nay: Hasan Nahid | Poem: Homa Mirafshar
Shotorbana | Oud and vocalist: Abdolvahab Shahidi |
Nay: Hasan Nahid | Poem: Mawlana Abdurrahman Jami

• Ghazalha (Lyrics) | Iraj in association with Ahmad

Produced by Ahange Rouz

Vocalist: Iraj and Ahmadi | Poem Mehdi Soheili
Side 1: Gol foroush (The Florist), Ghahvehchi (The Coffee shop owner), Rahgozar (The passer by) | Side 2: Miveh foroush (The fruit seller), Banna (The mason), Attarbashi (The herbalist)

• Azadeh'am (I am a free soul) | Nemidanam, nemikhaham bedanam (I don't know and I do not want to know)
Cover painting: Mohammad Tajvidi

Produced by Ahange Rouz

Azadeh'am (I am a free soul) | Vocalist: Hayedeh |
Composer: Ali Tajvidi | Poem: Rahi Moayyeri | Nemidanam, nemikhaham bedanam (I don't know and I do not want to know) | Vocalist: Hayedeh | Composer: Ali Tajvidi | Poem: Parviz Vakili

ماهی سیاه کوچولو

نوشته‌ی بهرنگ

بزی که گم شد

نوشته‌ی نادر ابراهیمی

قصه طوطی

شعر از م. آزاد

گل اومد بهار اومد

پیتر و گرگ

اثر پروکفیف

بابا برفی

شعر: جبار باغچه‌بان
موسیقی متن: احمد پژمان

قهرمان

نوشته: تقی کیارستمی
موسیقی متن: شیدا قرچه‌داغی

لی لی لی لی حوضک

نوشته‌ی م. آزاد

موسیقی متن: شیدا قرچه‌داغی

شاهزاده شاد

نوشته: اسکار وایلد
ترجمه‌ی: فریدون معزی مقدم

آهو و پرنده‌ها

نوشته‌ی نیما یوشیج
موسیقی متن: فریدون شهبازیان

انگشتری جادو

نوشته: کنستانتین پاستوفسکی
ترجمه‌ی: پوران صلح‌کل

- **Majmou'eye Seda baraye Koudakan (Collection of Voices for Children)**

Produced by the CIDCYA

- **Voices for Children 7 |** Ghahreman (The Champion)

Designer: Farshid Mesghali

Produced by the CIDCYA 1972

Story by Taghi Kiarostami | Music: Sheida Gharcheh Daghi Voices of Nikou Kheradmand : The Storyteller | Azar Daneshi: Zane Barzegar (The Farmer's wife) | Behzad Farahani: Pirmard (The Old Man) | Muzaffar Moghaddam: Barzigar (The Farmer) | Kioumars Mobashsheri: Derakh (The Tree) | Vafa Lahiji as the boy (the Champion) | Farah Kazemi as the Bolbol (Nightingale)

- **Voices for Children 2 |** Bozi ke gom shod (The goat who got lost)

Painting by Yuta Azargin

Produced by the CIDCYA 1971

Written by Nader Ebrahimi | Music: Esfandiar Monfaredzadeh | Voices of Maryam Mo'taref: Storyteller | Behzad Farahani: The Old Man | Babak: The Old Young Man | Iraj Adibzadeh: The Young Man | Muzaffar Moghaddam: The Young Man | Manijeh Fazeli: The Young Woman | Khosrow Farahzadi: The Young Man

- **Voices for Children 6 |** Baba Barfi (The Snow Father)

Cover design: Ahmad Asbaghi

Produced by the CIDCYA 1972

Story: Jabbar Baghtcheban | Music: Ahmad Pejman The voice of Fereydoun Daemi as the storyteller | Parviz Narenjiha : Baba Barfi | Iraj Pezeshkian as the Grandfather And children's voices: Morteza Joz'ei, Sonia Kholfi, Mehran Bakhshayesh, Farideh Kamalzadeh

پیتر و گرگ

قصه و موسیقی متن : سرگی پروکفیف

با صدای : فریدون دائمی

کانون پرورش فکری کودکان و نوجوانان
۱۳۵۰

● **Cover and back design for Voices for Children 5 |** Peter and the Wolf **Designer: Farshid Mesghali**

Produced by the CIDCYA 1971

Story and Music by Sergei Prokofiev | Voice of Fereydoun Daemi

پیتر و گرگ

اثر:
پروکفیف

طرح جلد از فرشید مثقالی ـ نقاشی عدنانی

• **Inside of the record of Voices for Children 8** | Li Li Li Li Howzak
Designer: Farshid Mesghali
Painting: Muhammad Adnani

Produced by the CIDCYA 1972

Written by M. Azad | Music: Sheida Gharcheh Daghi Voices of Nikou Kheradmand as the Storyteller | Parvin Chehrehnagar as the Bird | Shiva Gourani as the Chicken | Reza Babak as the Rooster | Ali Asghar Asgarian as the Crow | Sorayya Ghasemi as the Cat | Behzad Farahani as the Goat

کانون پرورش فکری کودکان و نوجوانان

تهران – ۱۳۵۲

۵ تومان

• Back design of the record of Children's Voices

Produced by the CIDCYA 1974

Arrangement of music: Hossein Alizadeh | Poem by Hamid Hamzeh

Hungarian Dance, Song of Brahms, One pieace | Behrouz Dabir Moghaddam, Mohsen Mesbahi

Kermanshahi Folk Song, Italian Folk Song, Bandari Folk Song, English Folk Song, Mojdeh | Hossein Alizadeh

The music of this record has been perfomed by the children of library 18 of the CIDCYA aged 8 to 12 years in Tehran.

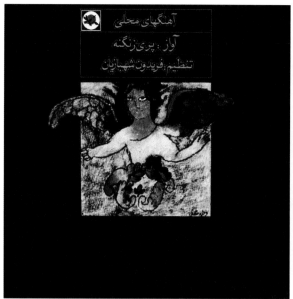

• Cover and back design of the record of Ahanghaye Mahalli (Folk Songs)
Designer: Farshid Mesghali

Produced by the CIDCYA 1974

Photograph: Masoud Masoumi | Arrangement by Fereydoun Shahbazian | Vocalist: Pari Zanganeh

• Pesarake Chashm Abi (The Blue-eyed Boy)
Painting: Farshid Mesghali

Produced by the CIDCYA 1974

Written by Javad Mojabi | Music: Kambiz Roshanravan Voices of Bijan Mofid, Siavash Tahmoures, Sousan Taslimi, Jamileh Nedaee, Alireza Mojallal, Mitra Ghamsari

• Selection of the Works of the CIDCYA

تنظیم موسیقی : اردشیر روحانی
ظالم ظالم
دوبدو
شیرنم سبزه
آگر باران
تنظیم موسیقی : شهداد روحانی
سیمای جان
تنظیم موسیقی : ۱ سماعیل تهرانی
دای بلال
جونی جونی
نسانسا
پاچ لیلی
بیجار کاره
اری وای
خروس خوان ، بدیور، سرکوی دوست :
پیانو اردشیر روحانی

● **Ahanghaye Mahalli (Folk Songs)** |
Vocalist: Minou Javan
Cover design: Bahram Khaef

Produced by the CIDCYA 1976

Music Arrangement: Ardeshir Rohani | Zalem Zalem
(Cruel cruel), Dobedo (Two by Two), Shirnam Sabzeh
(The moisture by milk grass), Agar baran (If rain...)
Music arrangement: Shahdad Rohani | Simaye jan
(The face of the soul)
Music arrangement: Esmail Tehrani | Dai Balal, Jooni
jooni, Nesa nesa, Pach Leili, Bijar Kareh, Ari van,
Khorous khan, Badivar, Sare kouye doost

تنظیم موسیقی:
کامبیز روشن روان
دختر بویراحمدی
شیری بگو سه تا
شیر علیمردان

آخ لیلم
هی یار هی یار
دمکل
شی ابوشیه
ای سرکنل
آسمان : پیانو اردشیر روحانی
تنظیم موسیقی : اسماعیل تهرانی
ترانه شیرازی
تنظیم موسیقی : اردشیر روحانی
شلیل

● **Ahanghaye Mahalli (Folk Songs) |**
Vocalist: Minou Javan
Cover design: Bahram Khaef

Produced by the CIDCYA 1976

Music arrangement: Kambiz Roshanravan | Dokhtare bouyer ahmadi, Shiri begoo seta, Shir Alimardan, Akh leylam, Hey yar hey yar, Domkal, Shi aboushiyeh, Ey sar Aseman (The Sky) | Piano: Ardeshir Rohani
Music arrangement: Esmail Tehrani | Taraneh Shirazi (The Shirazi Song)
Music arrangement: Ardeshir Rohani | Shalil (The Nectarine)

● Ahanghaye Mahalli (Folk Songs) |

Vocalist: Pari Zanganeh

Cover design: Farshid Mesghali

Produced by the CIDCYA 1976

Arrangement: Varouzhan
Shekare ahou, Dai balal, Karishim, Rashid kha, Dobedo,
Asmar asmar jan, Ghad boland to bio, Mastam mastam,
Baroon barooneh, Ey Leili

پارس فیلم تقدیم میکند

مهدی مشگی و شلوارک داغ

ناصر ملک مطیعی ، کریستین پاترسون

- **Mehdi Meshki va Shalvarake Dagh**
(The Black Mehdi and the Hot Shorts) |
Film Sound Track

Produced by Anoushirvan

Pars Film Presents | Naser Malek Motiee and Christian
Patterson | Director: Nezam Fatemi | Filming Director:
Mahmoud Koushan | Producer: Dr. Esmail Koushan |
Ki migeh (Who says), vocalist: Aref | Eshghe bipool (Love
with no money), vocalist: Ahdiyeh | Music: Homayoun
Khorram | Poem: Nezam Fatemi

- **Reza Motori (The Motorist Reza) | Farhad |** Film Sound Track

Produced by Ahange Rouz

Poem: Shahyar Ghanbari | Music: Esfandiar Monfaredzadeh

- **Bekhahi nakhahi hamineh (This is it, whether you want it or not) | Key miaee (When will you come) |** Film Sound Track

Produced by Olymic –
Trans Electric Manufacturing Company

Bekhahi nakhahi hamineh (This is it, whether you want it or not) | Sousan | Music: Parviz Atabaki | Poem: Shahyar
Key miaee (When will you come) by Sousan | Tajik | Music: Babak | Poem: Shahyar

- **Sound Tracks of the Hasan Kachal Film |** The first Persian Musical in Iran

Produced and disseminated by the Apolon Production and Industrial Factories

Producer: Ali Abbasi | Scenario writer and director: Ali Hatami
Reciters and vocalists: Ahdiyeh, Afshin, Nikou, Sousan, Esmaili, Mahtab, Kouros Sarhangzadeh | Dubbing: Mahrou | Music: Monfaredzadeh, Atabaki, Babak | Zarb: Bidarian
Recorded at the Tanin Studio by Mohammad Gorji

Chaprter Three

Typography

آهوی گردن دراز

نوشته‌ی جمشید سپهری
موسیقی شیداقرچه‌داغی

تهیه شده درکانون پرورش فکری کودکان و نوجوانان ۱۳۵۲

صدا: فرهاد. شعر: شهیارقنبری. آهنگ: واروژان

هفته خاکستری

غزلیات
مولوی

● **Hafteye Khakestari (The Grey Week) |**
Sedaee koutah baraye hamisheh seda
(A short sound for the eternal voice) for
Ahmad Shamlou
Design: Naderi
Calligrahpy: Mostafa Owji

Vocalist: Farhad | Poem: Shahyar Ghanbari | Music:
Varouzhan

• **Back design of the record of Poet's**
Voice 1 | Poems of Hafez of Shiraz
Designer: Farshid Mesghali
Calligraphy and painting: Mostafa Owji

Produced by the CIDCYA 1972

Hafez of Shiraz – Voica and Narration of Ahmad Shamlou |
Music: Feryedoun Shahbazian

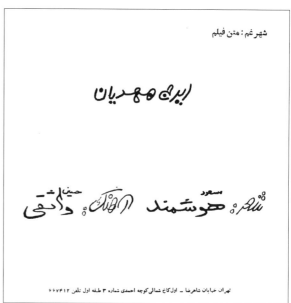

• Back design of the record of Shahre gham (The Town of Sorrow) | Film Sound Track

• Back design of the record of Shahre gham (The Town of Sorrow) | Film Sound Track

Produced by the Avaye Shahr Studio

Vocalist: Iraj Mahdian | Poem: Masoud Houshmand | Music: Hossein Vaseghi

• Back cover of the record of Salam Bar Eshgh (Hail to Love) | Bar nemigardam (I will not come back) | Iraj Mahdiank

Produced by the Avaye Shahr Studio

Vocalist: Iraj Mahdian | Poem: Masoud Houshmand | Salam Bar Eshgh (Hail to Love) | Poem and Music: Samad Nourian | Bar nemigardam (I will not come back) Poem and Music: Iraj Taheri

• Back cover of the record of Ghesseh (Story) | Gohare Yekdane (The Unique Pearl)

Produced by Royal Sourena

Ghesseh (Story) | Voice and music: Touraj | Poem: Shabod Arrangement: Eric
Gohare Yekdane (The Unique Pearl) | Voice and music: Touraj | Arrangement: Eric

• **Cover and back desigh of Poet's Voice 2** | Nima Youshij
Designer: Farshid Mesghali
Calligraphy: Mostafa Owji

Painting: Soudabeh Agah

Produced by the CIDCYA 1972

Poems of Nima Youshij recited by Ahmad Shamlou | Music: Ahmad Pejman

شعر نیما یوشیج با صدای احمد شاملو

موسیقی متن: احمد پژمان

نیما یوشیج

● **Poet's Voice 10 |** Poems of Sa'di recited by Houshang Ebtehaj
Design and painting: Farshid Mesghali
Produced by the CIDCYA 1973

Poems of Sa'di recited by Houshang Ebtehaj | Music: Fereydoun Shahbazian

● **Cover and back design of the record of Ahouye garden deraz (The Long Necked Deer)**
Painting: Ebrahim Haghighi
Produced by the CIDCYA 1973

Written by Jamshid Sepahi | Music: Sheida Gharcheh Daghi

- **Tangna (Predicament)** | Film Sound Track
Cover design: Esfand

Composer: Esfandiar Monfaredzadeh | Vocalist:
Fereydoun Foroughi | Poem: Farhad Sheibani

• **Poet's Voice 4** | Ghazaliyyate Mowlavi (Rumi's Lyrics) recited by Ahmad Shamlou **Design and implementation: Farshid Mesghali | Calligraphy: Mostafa Owji**

Produced by the CIDCYA 1972

Lyrics of Rumi recited by Ahmad Shamlou | Music: Fereydoun Shabazian

• **Cover and back design of the record of Poet's Voice 11** | Abu Saeed Abulkhayr **Designer: Mostafa Owji**

Produced by the CIDCYA 1974

Voice: Bijan Mofid | Music: Kambiz Roshanravan

• **Life and Works 10** | Aminollah Hossein
Cover design: Houshang Mohammadian
Painting: Bahram Khaef

Produced by the CIDCYA 1975

Edited by Arsalan Sasani | Written by Fereydoun Moezzi
Moghaddam | Voice of Aminollah Hossein

• Cover and back design of the record of Poet's Voice 1 | Poems of Hafez of Shiraz
Designer: Farshid Mesghali
Calligraphy and painting: Mostafa Owji

Produced by the CIDCYA 1972

Hafez of Shiraz recited and narrated by Ahmad Shamlou | Music: Fereydoun Shahbazian

● **Cover and back design of the Bon Bast (Dead End) record |** Dariush
Design: Iraj Nojoumi

Produced by Studio Phonetic, Sourena

Music and arrangement: Babak Bayat | Poem: Iraj Jannati Ataei | Vocalist: Dariush

• Inside page of Poet's Voice 4 |
Rumi's Lyrics
Design and implementation: Farshid Mesghali | Calligraphy: Mostafa Owji

Produced by the CIDCYA 1972

Rumi's Lyrics recited by Ahmad Shamlou | Music: Fereydoun Shahbazian

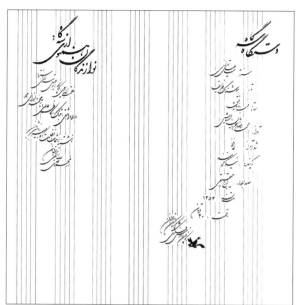

• Back design of the Segah record

Produced by the CIDCYA 1975

Written, selected and supervised by: Kambiz Roshanravan
Santour: Esmail Tehrani | Tar: Houshang Zarif | Setar:
Mehrbanou Tofigh
Vocalist: Mohammad Reza Shajarian | Poem of chants:
Hafez | Reciter: Nikou Kheradmand | Recorder; Iraj Haghighi
Co-players of Segah | Rahmatullah Badiee: Kamancheh
Esmail Tehrani: Santour | Davoud Vaseghi: Tombak |
Kazem Alemi: Tar | Mohammad Delnavazi: Oud

• Inside of the record of Voices for Children 8 | Li Li Li Li Howzak

Produced by the CIDCYA 1972

Written by M. Azad | Music: Sheida Gharcheh Daghi
Voices of Nikou Kheradmand as the Storyteller | Parvin
Chehrehnagar as the Bird | Shiva Gourani as the Chicken
Reza Babak as the Rooster | Ali Asghar Asgarian as the
Crow | Sorayya Ghasemi as the Cat | Behzad Farahani
as the Goat

• Back design of Poet's Voice 4 |
Rumi's Lyrics
Design and implementation: Farshid Mesghali | Calligraphy: Mostafa Owji

Produced by the CIDCYA 1972

Rumi's Lyrics recited by Ahmad Shamlou | Music:
Fereydoun Shahbazian

- **Aseman migeryad emshab (The sky weeps tonight) | Ghame tanhaee (The pain of loneliness)**
Designer: Andre

Stereofonic production at Ahange Rouz

Sitar: Mehrpouyai

- **Cover and back design of Poet's Voice 12 |** Poems of Baba Taher
Designer: Mostafa Owji

Produced by the CIDCYA 1974

Vocalist: Pari Zanganeh | Reciter: Amir Nouri | Music: Sheida Gharcheh Daghi

● Do ta chashme siah dari (You have two black eyes) | Na dige (Not anymore)

Produced by Ahange Rouz

Music, poem and singing: Bijan Mofid

- **Chahargah**
Cover design: Farshi Mesghalii

Produced by the CIDCYA 1975

Written, selected and supervised by Kambiz Roshanravan

● Back cover of the Naghmeye Esfahan (Esfahan Song) record | Rastpanjgah Cover design: Farshid Mesghali

Produced by the CIDCYA 1975

Written, selected and supervised by: Kambiz Roshanravan
Vocalist: Mohammad Reza Shajarian | Poem of chants: Mowlavi | Reciter: Nikou Kheradmand | Recorder: Iraj Haghighi

Santour: Esmail Tehrani | Tar: Houshang Zarif | Setar: Mehrbanou Tofigh
Vocalist: Mohammad Reza Shajarian | Poem of chants: Hafez | Reciter: Nikou Kheradmand | Recorder; Iraj Haghighi
Santour: Esmail Tehrani | Tar: Houshang Zarif | Setar: Mehrbanou Tofigh | Kamancheh: Rahatullah Badiee | Oud: Mohammad Delnavazi
Co-players of the Esfahan Song | Rahmatullah Badiee: Kamancheh | Esmail Tehrani: Santour
Davoud Vaseghi: Tombak | Kazem Alemi: Tar | Mohammad Delnavazi: Oud

Printed in Great Britain
by Amazon